All About Florida

People, Places, Facts, and Things
Everyone Needs to Know

SWEETWATER
PRESS

Contents

THE BASICS

Just the Facts

- Florida became a state on March 3, 1845, making it the twenty-seventh state in the U.S.

- The word Florida means "Flowery Easter" in Spanish.

- Today, Florida has the second highest population of any Southern state. (Only Texas has more people.) It used to be that Florida had the lowest population of any Southern state, but that changed as tourism trends changed in the twentieth century.

- Florida ranks fourth in the country in terms of state population.

- There are 275 zip codes in Florida.

- Almost 18,000,000 people live in Florida.

- The state has an area of 58,560 miles: 54,136 squares miles are land and 4,424 square miles are water.

- From north to south, the state is 447 miles long.

- A peninsula, Florida is nearly surrounded by three bodies of water: the Straits of Florida, the Gulf of Mexico, and the Atlantic Ocean.

- Florida is bordered by two other states—Alabama and Georgia.

- Florida has the second longest coastline in the country. (Alaska comes in first, but its beach tourism doesn't exactly compare!)

- Tallahassee is the capital of Florida.

- Jacksonville is the biggest city in Florida.

- Florida's nickname is "The Sunshine State."

- Fort Meade was established during the Seminole Indian Wars. It is the oldest part of Polk County, dating to 1849.

Did You Know?

- Hernando County was originally named Benton County from 1844-1850.
- Bradford County was originally named New River from 1858-1861.

- Each county was named after something or someone significant. Can you name all the counties? Do you know what your county is named after?

County	Established	Named After
Alachua	1824	Named after the Native American word for "sinkhole"
Baker	1861	Named after Confederate Senator James McNair Baker
Bay	1913	Named after St. Andrews Bay
Bradford	1861	Named after Captain Richard Bradford of the Civil War
Brevard	1855	Named after either Theodore Washington Brevard or Doctor Ephraim Brevard
Broward	1915	Named after Governor Napoleon Bonaparte Broward
Calhoun	1838	Named after South Carolina Senator John Calhoun
Charlotte	1921	Named after the Bay of Charlotte Harbor
Citrus	1887	Named for the citrus industry

County	Established	Named After
Clay	1858	Named after U.S. Senator Henry Clay (KY)
Collier	1923	Named after developer Barron Collier
Columbia	1832	Named after Christopher Columbus
DeSoto	1887	Named after Spanish explorer Hernando de Soto
Dixie	1921	Refers to a nickname of the South
Duval	1822	Named after Territorial Governor William P. DuVal
Escambia	1821	Named after the Escambia River, which comes from the Spanish word "to barter"
Flagler	1917	Named after railroad mogul Henry M. Flagler
Franklin	1832	Named after Benjamin Franklin
Gadsden	1823	Named after James Gadsden

County	Established	Named After
Gilchrist	1925	Named after Governor Albert W. Gilchrist
Glades	1921	Named after the Florida Everglades
Gulf	1925	Named after the Gulf of Mexico
Hamilton	1827	Named after Secretary of Treasury Alexander Hamilton
Hardee	1921	Named after Governor Cary A. Hardee
Hendry	1923	Named after settler Captain Francis A. Hendry
Hernando	1843	Named after Spanish explorer Hernando de Soto
Highlands	1921	Named for the terrain
Hillsborough	1834	Named after Wills Hill of England
Holmes	1848	Named after settler Thomas J. Holmes from North Carolina

County	Established	Named After
Indian River	1925	Named after the Indian River
Jackson	1822	Named after President Andrew Jackson
Jefferson	1827	Named after President Thomas Jefferson
Lafayette	1856	Named after the American Revolution's Marquis de Lafayette, a French officer
Lake	1887	Named after the county's large number of lakes
Lee	1887	Named after Robert E. Lee
Leon	1824	Named after Juan Ponce de Leon
Levy	1845	Named after U.S. Senator David Levy
Liberty	1855	Named after the American dream of liberty
Manatee	1855	Named after the animal

County	Established	Named After
Marion	1844	Named after Francis Marion, a general in the Revolutionary War
Martin	1925	Named after Governor John W. Martin
Miami-Dade	1836	Named after army Major Francis L. Dade
Monroe	1823	Named after President James Monroe
Nassau	1824	Named after the Duchy of Nassau
Okaloosa	1915	Named after the Choctaw Indian words for "water" and "black"
Okeechobee	1917	Named after the Hitchiti Indian words for "water" and "big"
Orange	1845	Named after the orange industry
Osceola	1887	Named after Indian leader Osceola
Palm Beach	1909	Named after the county's trees and sandy beaches

County	Established	Named After
Pasco	1887	Named after U.S. Senator Samuel Pasco
Pinellas	1911	Named after the Spanish phrase "Pinta Pinal" which means "Point of Pines"
Polk	1861	Named after President James K. Polk
Putnam	1849	Named after either Israel Putnam of the Revolutionary War or Benjamin A. Putnam of the Seminole War
St. Johns	1821	Named after St. John the Baptist
St. Lucie	1844	Named after St. Lucie of Syracuse, a Roman Catholic saint
Santa Rosa	1842	Named after Roman Catholic saint Rosa de Viterbo
Sarasota	1921	Named after the Indian word for "not known"
Seminole	1913	Named after the Seminole Indians

County	Established	Named After
Sumter	1853	Named after General Thomas Sumter of the Revolutionary War
Suwannee	1858	Named after the Cherokee word for "echo river"
Taylor	1856	Named after President Zachary Taylor
Union	1921	Named after Unity
Volusia	1854	Named after English settler Volus
Wakulla	1843	Named after an Indian word possibly meaning "spring of water"
Walton	1824	Named after George Walton, the Secretary of Territorial Florida in the 1820s
Washington	1825	Named after President George Washington

It's Official!

Over the years, Florida has adopted many different objects to represent the state. Did you know that each of the following is a symbol of Florida?

- State Motto: "In God We Trust"

- State Song: "Old Folks at Home (Suwanee River)"
  (Interestingly enough, Stephen Foster, who wrote the state song, never even visited Florida!)

- State Bird: Mockingbird

- State Flower: Orange Blossom

- State Gem: Moonstone

Did You Know?

Ironically, the moonstone is not found naturally in Florida—or on the moon.

Did You Know?

The alligator originally symbolized Florida's extensive untamed wilderness and swamps.

- State Reptile: Alligator
- State Animal: Florida Panther
- State Insect: Zebra Longwing Butterfly
- State Marine Animal: Manatee (also known as the "sea cow")
- State Saltwater Mammal: Porpoise
- State Freshwater Fish: Largemouth Bass
- State Saltwater Fish: Atlantic sailfish
- State Shell: Horse Conch
- State Play: *Cross and Sword*, which depicts the story of the Spanish colonization of St. Augustine.
- State Tree: Sabal Palm

- State Drink: Orange Juice

- State Fruit: Orange

- State Pie: Key Lime Pie

- State Wildflower: Coreopsis

- State Stone: Agatized Coral

Did You Know?

Agatized coral occurs when silica in the ocean water hardens, replacing the limy corals with a form of quartz known as chalcedony. Scientists believe this process takes millions of years to complete.

- State Soil: Myakka Fine Sand. Myakka means "Big Waters" in Native American languages. It's a native soil of Florida and isn't found in any other state. It is wet and sandy.

- State Band: St. Johns River City Band

THE GREAT
OUTDOORS

Natural Landmarks

- Ninety-five percent of Biscayne National Park is water. The park preserves Biscayne Bay, which is one of the top scuba diving areas in the U.S. The shore of the bay is the location of an extensive mangrove forest.

- St. Augustine is home to the supposed "Fountain of Youth."

- One of the two naturally round lakes in the world is found at DeFuniak Springs.

Biscayne National Park
Photo by John Brooks
Courtesy of NPS

Did You Know?

Biscayne National Park and Everglades National Park are both in Miami. Miami is the only city in the country with two national parks nearby.

- Bok Tower stands at 205 feet, overlooking a reflection pool. At Bok Tower Gardens, you can find beautiful gardens, a nature preserve, and a 20-room Mediterranean Revival mansion on the 250-acre beauty.

- One of the most beautiful gardens in the world can be found in Cypress Gardens. Dick Pope Sr. designed the gardens over seventy years ago!

- Key Largo is the biggest island in the Florida Keys, and the one that's farthest north.

- Speaking of the Florida Keys, the seven-mile bridge there is the longest bridge in the state.

- The oldest city in North America is St. Augustine.

- Ft. Lauderdale has a rather interesting nickname. It's known as the "Venice of the America." (That's a comparison to Venice, Italy, in case you weren't sure.)

Seven Mile Bridge
Courtesy of VISIT FLORIDA

Did You Know?

- Key West is the hottest city in the country!
- The highest point in the state is Britton Hill, which is 345 feet above sea level.
- Lakeland, Florida, got its name from the nineteen lakes that are within its city limits.

- Florida Caverns State Park, located just north of Marianna, is the only Florida state park to offer cave tours to the public. The caverns have stunning formations of limestone stalactites and stalagmites.

Florida Caverns
Courtesy of VISIT FLORIDA

- Although it might come as quite a surprise, Hawaii is the southernmost state in the U.S.—not Florida. However, the southernmost city in the U.S. is in Florida.

- Tarpon Springs is known for its sponge docks.

- Lake Okeechobee is the biggest lake in Florida.

- Florida has a few things backwards. St. Johns River flows north instead of south. There are very few rivers that do that!

- There are two rivers by the same name in Florida—there is a Withlacoochee in both north and central Florida.

- Benwood is a shipwreck on the French Reef in the Florida Keys. It is considered one of the most popular sites for divers.

- The Hawthorne Trail, part of Florida's Rails to Trails program, is seventeen miles long!

- "Spoil Island" off Port Manatee was created in the late 1960s out of silt dug from the ocean to create shipping channels.

- Everglades National Park was visited by nearly 1.2 million people in 2004.

- Elliott Key is the park's largest island and is considered the first of the true Florida Keys.

- The Everglades are subtropical marshlands located in southern Florida. Elevated areas of the Everglades contain a number of trees, namely cypress and red mangrove. Water from the Everglades is used as water supply for major cities in the area.

- Everglades National Park preserves the southern portion of the Everglades but represents only 20 percent of the wetland area. The park contains a number of trails, the most famous being the Anhinga Trail, which allows close views of various types of birds, including heron and anhinga.

- Big Cypress National Preserve, which borders Everglades National Park, has served as home to Native Americans such as the Seminoles and Miccosukee. It later was home to early settlers of the area, a timber industry, and alligator poachers.

Big Cypress National Preserve
Courtesy of NPS

- Big Cypress is the most biologically diverse region of the terrestrial Everglades, housing birds, trees, alligators, venomous snakes, and the Florida panther.

- Located within Bill Baggs State Park and Recreation area, the Cape Florida Lighthouse rises on the southernmost tip of Key Biscayne. The lighthouse was built in 1825 and attacked by Seminoles in 1836. When rebuilt in 1855, the height of the tower was extended 65 feet. A climb to the top of the 95-foot tower offers a beautiful view of the surrounding island and sea.

Cape Florida Lighthouse
Courtesy of VISIT FLORIDA

- Florida began developing its underwater parks in 1987, and today they feature a number of shipwrecks and other historic sites. Each site is named with an underwater plaque, and scuba divers can get laminated maps to help them find these locations at local dive shops. These sites include:

Urca de Lima – Opened September 1987 – Shipwreck of a Spanish fleet that sank in a 1715 hurricane off the coast of Ft. Pierce.

San Pedro – Opened April 1989 – A ship from the 1733 Spanish Plate Fleet wrecked in the Florida Keys.

City of Hawkinsville – Opened 1992 – A Suwannee River steamboat that sunk in the 1920s.

USS *Massachusetts* – Opened June 1993 – 350-foot long battleship under Pensacola Pass.

Lofthus – A merchant ship that used to travel the world and battle pirates, and wrecked off the coast of Manalapan in 1898.

Flora and Fauna

- Wild flamingos are only found in Florida.

- Flamingos get their coloring from their food. They are pink because their diet consists mainly of shrimp. The pinker a flamingo is, the more shrimp it has been feasting on!

- Bottlenose dolphins born in the waters of Florida are smaller than the same breed of dolphin born off the coast of England.

- Gurnards are fish that grunt when thunderstorms are approaching. They are native to Florida.

- Walking catfish can live for up to eighty days on land.

- A stingray's barbed spine, which occasionally injects poison into the feet of swimmers who accidentally step on it, is usually ineffective against sharks, the stingray's main predator.

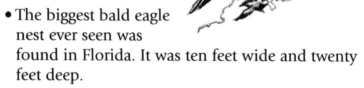

- Most seagulls, otherwise known as gulls, feed on crabs and small fish.

- The first porpoise born in captivity was born on Valentine's Day 1990 in Marineland, Florida.

- The biggest bald eagle nest ever seen was found in Florida. It was ten feet wide and twenty feet deep.

- There are more palm trees in Florida than anywhere else in North America.

- As far as the U.S. goes, the Everglades are only found in Florida.

- You better bring your Off! when you visit Florida. There are sixty species of mosquitos here.

- There is an entire museum in Gainesville dedicated to Fred Bear, a man who promoted the management of wildlife and founded Bear Archery Company.

- There are forty-five species of snakes in Florida, but only six are venomous and dangerous—Eastern Coral Snake, Dusky Pygmy Rattlesnake, Timber Rattlesnake, Eastern Diamondback Rattlesnake, Cottonmouth, and Southern Copperhead.

- Fruit & Spice Park in Homestead, Florida, is the only tropical botanical garden of its kind in the U.S. There, botanists grow more than five hundred varieties of fruits, vegetables, herbs, nuts, and spices from around the world. It grows sixty-five different kinds of bananas and forty different kinds of grapes.

- Florida has more than 4,100 species of native ferns and seed plants. It is third in the country for its floral diversity.

- According to the Exotic Pest Plant Council of Florida, "native" plants were already in the state when the Europeans landed there around 1500. The group is concerned that plants moved into the state (invasive exotic plants) will grow out of control and mess up the balance of "plant communities" in nature.

- According to the University of South Florida, nearly one out of three plants in Florida is non-native.

- Aquatic Plants of Florida, Inc. is the largest producer of sea oats in the state.

- Aquatic Plants of Florida, Inc. once tried to organize a boycott of Cypress mulch with a posting on their website, "Why kill a tree to grow a flower?" listing reasons why the brand wasn't good for the state of Florida.

- Florida wetland plants are divided into four categories:

  - Emergent Plants – Rooted in soil and growing both above and below the surface of water

  - Submerged Plants – Grow entirely below water

  - Floating-leaved Plants – Float on the surface of water, such as water lilies

  - Floating Plants – Unattached at the roots and suspended in the water, such as water lettuce

- Florida is often associated with shark attacks. There are about 375 species of sharks in the world.

Worldwide, there are about 50 to 70 shark attacks a year.

- If you hear a big splat on your car window driving through Florida, it's probably a love bug. When they're mating, love bugs (also known as Bibinoid Flies) don't pay very good attention and tend to end up on windshields.

- Swamps, such as those found in the Everglades, function in three ways: their vegetation serves as a filter to clean water, they are a major habitat for wildlife and plant life, and they prevent flooding by slowing down the flow of water after heavy rains.

Did You Know?

Florida is the winter home of most of eastern North America's birds.

Beach Facts

- Seashells were originally used as currency in Papua New Guinea until 1933.

- Male seahorses become pregnant, not the females. They have a gestation period of two to three weeks. Up to 20 million seahorses are captured every year to be used in herbology.

- Ponte Vedra Beach is home to the PGA Tour and The Players Championship.

- CNN and *Money Magazine* once listed Ponte Vedra Beach as one of the fifty best places to live in the U.S.

- The Atlantic Ocean is the world's second-largest ocean and covers one-fifth of the earth's surface.

- The deepest part of the Gulf of Mexico is about three hundred nautical miles and is called Sigsbee Deep, or "Grand Canyon under the Sea."

- The pollution of the ocean has more than doubled since 1950.

- Jacksonville Beach was originally called Ruby Beach.

- Hudson Beach in Pasco County is one of the country's largest artificial canal cities.

- The study of sand is called "arenology."

- Because the city was so small, Indian Harbour Beach's first fire truck cost $750 and the original police chief had to use his personal car for patrols.

- A "dune field" is an area covered extensively by sand dunes.

- When a blue flag flies by the shoreline, the waters are safe for swimming.

- Miami Beach is one of the top destinations for gay tourism in the U.S.

- Cocoa Beach was the setting for *I Dream of Jeannie* in the 1960s, but only one episode was actually filmed on site.

- Fort Walton Beach is home to the annual Billy Bowlegs Pirate Festival, which is similar to Mardi Gras.

- In beach volleyball, it is not against the rules to go under the net as long as it doesn't interfere with the other team's attempt to play the ball.

- On average, Florida has three hundred days of sunshine per year.

- Navarre Beach, Florida, has been hit by four hurricanes in eleven years. In 2006, the city added one hundred feet of fresh sand to the beach as a part of a "renourishment" project.

Did You Know?

A museum in Sanibel, which owns 2 million shells, claims to be the world's only museum devoted solely to mollusks.

STATE HISTORY

Early Beginnings

- Some historians believe that Florida's first permanent settlement was formed at Atlantic Beach near the St. Johns River in 3570 BC.

- Various Native American tribes probably occupied Florida for twelve thousand years before the land was re-discovered by European explorers.

- These indigenous peoples included the Ais, the Apalachee, the Calusa, the Timucua, and the Tocobago tribes.

- Evidence of pre-Columbian artifacts, as well as an ancient Indian village, can be found at Crane Point Hammock in Marathon. This 63.5 acres of land is one of the most important historical and archaeological sites in the Florida Keys.

- Juan Ponce de Leon claimed Florida for the Spanish in 1513. He named the land

"Pascua Florida" because he discovered it "in the time of the Feast of Flowers," or Easter.

- Many historians believe Ponce de Leon wasn't the first European to reach Florida because at least one Indian with which he came in contact could already speak Spanish.

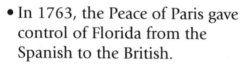

- While Hernando de Soto was searching for the fountain of youth in 1539, he came across Espiritu Santo Springs, which have attracted worldwide attention for their curative powers.

- In 1763, the Peace of Paris gave control of Florida from the Spanish to the British.

- But, twenty years later, the English would lose control of Florida again, and the territory would fall back into Spanish hands.

- Between 1817 and 1818, U.S. settlers battled Creek natives as well as people from Spain and Great Britain for ownership over the land. General Andrew Jackson burned many Native American villages during this time.

- In 1819, the U.S. became the official power over Florida.

- Osceola was a defiant young leader of the Seminoles in their resistance to Indian emigration. In 1935, he stuck his knife into the treaty he was asked to sign that would move his people to the West.

- Osceola's action led to the Second Seminole War, which started in Bushnell, Florida, on December 28, 1835.

- Florida officially became a state in 1845.

The Civil War

- In 1860, 61,745 individuals in the state of Florida were in bondage as slaves.

- Florida seceded from the Union on January 10, 1861, by a vote of 62-7.

- Ten days later, Florida became a founding member of the Confederate States of America.

- Fort Zachary Taylor was active during the U.S. Civil War, the Spanish-American War, World War I, and World War II. The fort was built between 1845 and 1866. Successful Union operations at the fort are credited with shortening the Civil War.

- Olustee Battlefield State Park is where the largest Civil War battle in the state of Florida was fought.

- Although Florida provided Confederate troops with salt, beef, pork, and cotton, more than two thousand Floridians joined the Union army.

- Florida is the only Southern state whose capital was not captured by the Union during the Civil War.

- Florida provided fifteen thousand troops for the Confederacy, organized into twelve infantry regiments, two cavalry regiments, and several artillery batteries.

- Despite the rest of Florida's stance during the Civil War, Key West was considered to be on the North's side.

- On June 25, 1868, Florida officially rejoined the United States after the South's defeat in the Civil War.

World War II

- More than a quarter of a million Floridians were drafted into World War II.

- More than six hundred thousand men trained in south Florida.

- German prisoner of war camps were located in Kendall and Homestead.

- During World War II, four German agents were caught paddling into Florida on a rubber raft from a submarine.

- During World War II, hotels in Clearwater were turned into barracks for new army recruits—including the luxurious and historic Fort Harrison Hotel and Belleview Biltmore. The government paid hotel owners $20 per soldier per month.

- Clearwater used blackouts to confuse potential enemy bombers during the night.

- During World War II, more than twenty thousand pilots were trained at the Naval Air Station in

Jacksonville ("NAS Jax"), which was the first naval installation in the city.

- During the war, there were rumors that German spies were infiltrating the theatres in Miami.

- The *Portero del Llano* was attacked by a German submarine off Miami Beach, burned, and sank on May 19, 1942.

- Florida beaches and golf courses were used to train troops because tourists no longer frequented the area—they wouldn't travel because of the rationing of gasoline, oil, and tires.

- The Miami Beach Servicemen's Pier was a popular spot for dancing, swimming, fishing, Spanish lessons, ping-pong, music, and more. Celebrities like Rita Hayworth and Bob Hope made appearances at the pier to cheer on the troops.

More History

- In 1899, Florida adopted its official state flag.

- Contrary to popular belief, the Civil Rights movement did not begin in Alabama—it began in Jacksonville in the 1910s when African Americans boycotted the segregation on public transportation. In turn, the city repealed the Jim Crow laws. However, the governor ordered they be put back in place. In 1960, on a day known as "Ax Handle Saturday," members of the Ku Klux Klan used ax handles and baseball bats to attack civil rights protestors at a peaceful sit-in at a restaurant.

Did You Know?

Asa Philip Randolph, who grew up in Jacksonville, was one of the most visible spokesmen for African-American civil rights and was a founder of the Harlem magazine <u>The Messenger</u>.

- Key West's biggest natural disaster was the Labor Day Hurricane in 1935, which decimated Key West's railroads and killed hundreds of residents.

- Florida's most fatal hurricane was on September 15, 1928, killing nearly two thousand people. Because many of these people were nomads, the exact toll was never known.

- Hurricane Andrew struck Florida on August 24, 1992. At that time it was the second costliest weather disaster in U.S. history.

- In 2004, Florida was hit by four hurricanes: Charley, Frances, Ivan, and Jeanne. 2005 proved to be no picnic either as Dennis, Katrina, Rita, and Wilma slammed into the state.

Did You Know?

The 1935 hurricane memorial, called the Florida Keys Memorial, remembers those lost in the storm. A crypt inside the monument holds the remains of many of the victims.

- In 1982, Key West seceded from the United States. Residents of Key West objected to federal regulations on the inspection of vehicles entering and leaving the Keys. Key West referred to itself as "The Conch Republic" during this time. The republic's saying was, "We secede where others failed."

- The Great Fire of 1901 devastated the city of Cleaveland while workers were on their lunch break. Ten thousand people were homeless after eight hours of fighting the fire.

- When the British took over Florida in the mid 1700s, the state was divided into two sections—East Florida, with a capital in St. Augustine; and West Florida, with a capital in Pensacola. When the land was finally deemed a territory of the United States, the two sides merged and named a new capital— Tallahassee, which was half way between the original two cities.

- President Andrew Jackson spent $20 million getting the Seminoles off the land that would be Florida.

- Florida's earliest shipwreck site was discovered in 1992 on Pensacola Bay. It was a Colonial Spanish ship and more than three thousand artifacts were recovered. The ship was likely a part of Tristan de Luna's trip to try and colonize the state in 1559. A hurricane destroyed many of his ships anchored in the Bay.

- Jacksonville was the busiest military port in the country during the first Gulf War (1991).

- Florida is home to a number of famous historical war forts. They include:

  – Fort Clinch (Fernandina Beach) – Civil War Fort

  – Fort Pickens (Pensacola Beach) – Civil War Fort that once held prisoner Geronimo

  – Fort Caroline (Jacksonville) – A replica of a 1564 French colony

  – Castillo de San Marcos National Monument (Saint Augustine) – Spanish Prison to supporters of the American Revolution

Castillo de San Marcos National Monument
Courtesy of VISIT FLORIDA

Did You Know?

Castillo de San Marcos is made of a stone called coquina, which means little shells. Construction on the fort was completed in 1695, after twenty-three years.

- In 2000, after droughts dried up some of Florida's lakes, nineteenth-century canoes were discovered in Newnan's Lake near Gainesville. Nearly ninety were uncovered in the mud.

- The oldest canoes to ever be discovered in Florida were found in DeLon Springs—they were dated about six thousand years old.

- Thousands of years ago, the Florida peninsula was likely twice the size it is today due to rising water levels.

- There have never been dinosaur remains found in Florida. This is because it was not a land mass at the time of the dinosaur—it was underwater.

Florida Firsts

- Florida's first schoolteachers were Franciscan friars.

- Oranges were first grown by settlers in St. Augustine in 1579.

- Florida's first constitution was drafted in 1838 by representatives from each county. The group wrote the document in anticipation of being officially named a state.

- There's probably at least one reason dads everywhere like Florida—the first U.S. golf course was built here.

- The State Board of Health was first developed during the yellow fever outbreak of 1889.

- The first night flight took place by Lincoln Beachy at Tampa.

- The first African American woman circuit judge was Melvia Green of Dade County.

- The first riding lawn mower, made by Snapper, was invented by the Smith brothers of Montverde, Florida.

- Florida's first neo-natal care unit was developed in 1960 at Shands HealthCare.

- Florida is home to the world's first underwater hotel.

- Florida's first resort was in the city of Fernandina Beach in the mid nineteenth-century. President James Monroe called it a "festering fleshpot."

- Florida's first blizzard was the Great Blizzard of 1899. To this date, it is the only time the temperature has ever dropped below zero degrees Fahrenheit.

- Amelia Earhart left on the first leg of her round-the-world flight from Miami. Her plane disappeared over the Pacific Ocean just a month later.

- The first woman to ever perform the duties of a Jewish rabbi in the United States was Paula Ackerman, a Pensacola native who led services at Beth-El Temple in Pensacola.

- Alan Shepard, the first American astronaut, was launched into space from Cape Canaveral.

- Aviator Tony Jannus flew the world's first scheduled passenger airplane from St. Petersburg to Tampa on January 1, 1914.

- People from Alabama and Georgia first began vacationing in Panama City Beach in the 1830s. The city wasn't named until 1909.

- You can thank Apalachicola's Dr. John Gorrie for keeping all of your food from spoiling. He invented the mechanical refrigeration process in 1851.

- Miami Beach pharmacist Benjamin Green invented sunscreen in 1944 by heating cocoa butter in a coffee pot.

- The city of Miami installed the first ATM that caters specifically to rollerbladers.

- The first graded road ever built in Florida was Old Kings Road (1763), named for King George of England.

- Florida's first railroad was built by Henry Flagler.

- One of Florida's first resorts for African Americans was American Beach, built during segregation in 1935.

- The Morikami Museum and Japanese Gardens at Delray Beach is the only museum in the U.S. dedicated exclusively to the living culture of Japan.

- In 1982, the orange crops were ruined thanks to "Cold Sunday," which saw freezing conditions throughout the country.

COMMERCE
AND TRADE

State Crops & Industries

- It isn't just something you see in commercials—Florida thrives on oranges! In fact, oranges are the biggest selling crop in Florida.

- Coca-Cola's Minute Maid brand was ecstatic when Ben Hill Griffin of Frostproof, Florida, received ten acres of land as a wedding present and turned it into a million-dollar piece of property. With the help of only one other man—who only had one arm—Griffin cleared the woods and planted citrus trees. His land became the company's main source of oranges.

- The top counties that produce citrus are St. Lucie, Polk, Henry, Highlands, Indian River, and Desoto.

- Forty percent of the oranges were once thrown out because they were bruised or damaged.

- In 1929 much of the citrus industry was destroyed by the Mediterranean fruit fly. Roadblocks were set up along the highways to check vehicles for contraband fruit, and the citrus production dropped by 60 percent.

- Florida's second largest industry is agriculture, namely citrus fruits.

- In 2006, 67 percent of all citrus, 74 percent of oranges, 54 percent of grapefruit, and 58 percent of tangerines grown in the U.S. were produced in Florida.

- Sugarcane and celery are among the other major crops grown in the state.

- Most students would be lost without Cedar Key. That city provides the wood from which pencils are made!

- Hospitality is a booming business in Florida. Tourists bring lots of money to the state when they visit its many beaches and amusement parks.

- In the past, Florida was known for agriculture and cattle farming.

- In the 1870s, steamboat tours down Florida rivers were a popular tourist attraction.

- Miami is the number one cruise port in the world.

- Commercial fishing is vital to Florida's economy.

- Most of the shrimp in Florida are found in the waters off Amelia Island. Eighty percent of Florida's shrimp come from there.

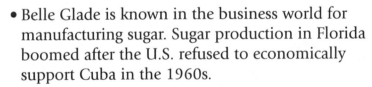

- Banking and phosphate mining also help drive the state.

- Florida does not have an income tax.

- Belle Glade is known in the business world for manufacturing sugar. Sugar production in Florida boomed after the U.S. refused to economically support Cuba in the 1960s.

- Florida has six veteran's hospitals—Tampa, Lake City, St. Petersburg, West Palm Beach, Miami, and Gainsville.

- Ybor City was once known as the Cigar Capital of the World. At one point it had nearly twelve thousand employees making cigars in two hundred different factories.

- Since the arrival of the NASA Merritt Island launch sites on Cape Canaveral in 1962, Florida has developed quite an aerospace industry.

- Every time an astronaut goes into space, Florida is in the news. That's because Cape Canaveral provides the launch pad for NASA.

Did You Know?

Titusville, located on the western shore of the Indian River directly across from the Kennedy Space Center, is known as Space City, USA.

ARTS AND LITERATURE

Musicians

Florida has given birth to its fair share of musicians over the years!

- Even though Ray Charles (1930-2004) was born in Georgia, he grew up in Gainesville, Florida. Ray began to lose his sight at the age of five and was completely blind by the time he was seven. Even though very poor, Ray learned to read Braille and play many different musical instruments. Over the rest of his career, Ray would continue to grow in prominence and recognition for songs like "Georgia on my Mind," "Hit the Road, Jack," and "America the Beautiful." In 2005, Jamie Foxx won an Oscar for best actor for his portrayal of Ray in the film *Ray*.

- Born in 1934 in Jacksonville, Florida, Pat Boone was a popular teenage singer and star of the fifties. He hit the charts with a version of "Ain't That a Shame" and also had hits with "Don't Forbid Me" and "Love Letters in the Sand." As the Beatles and other bands began to change the face of American rock and roll, Pat faded off the pop culture radar. Today, Pat is primarily influential in his church and family and prefers to champion conservative causes when given the opportunity to discuss politics.

- The Doors was a very popular band in the 1960s, and the group's lead singer, Jim Morrison, was a Florida native. Jim was born in 1943 in Melbourne. Songs like "Light my Fire" and "Break on Through" quickly took The Doors to the top of the charts. However, Jim's struggles with alcohol and drug abuse were the personal demons he could not overcome. He died in 1971 in Paris, France. But, his music lives on, and you might have seen Val Kilmer's portrayal of Jim in the 1991 movie *The Doors*.

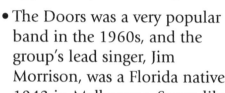

- An entertainer during the "Golden Age of Radio," Frances Langford was born in Lakeland, Florida, and made her rise as a big band singer during the 1930s. She performed regularly on Dick Powell's radio show and made several film appearances in movies such as *Yankee Doodle Dandy* (1942) and *Born to Dance* (1936). Her most popular song was "I'm in the Mood for Love." She hosted two variety shows, *Frances Langford Presents* and *The Frances Langford Show.* She moved to Jensen Beach, Florida, after marrying her second husband. She died at that home at the age of ninety-two.

- Backstreet Boy A.J. McLean (Alexander James McLean Fernandez) was born in West Palm Beach in 1978. He moved to Orlando at the age of twelve to pursue a career in acting and singing. After auditioning for shows on Nickelodeon, he landed a gig on *Welcome Freshmen* and the comedy show *Hi Honey! I'm Home.* He was recruited at age fourteen to join the new group The Backstreet Boys by producer Lou Pearlman. Today he has more than thirty-five tattoos and has established a foundation to raise money for diabetes research. He occasionally performs in New York clubs under the surname Johnny No Name when he is not with the group.

Did You Know?

Tom Petty of "Tom Petty and the Heartbreakers" is from Gainesville, Florida.

- Another Backstreet Boy, Howie Dorough, was born in Orlando. His show biz debut was at age six in a local performance of *The Wizard of Oz*. Howie went on to star in many high school productions and appeared in several Nickelodeon productions before joining The Backstreet Boys.

- Born in 1928 in Tampa, Julian "Cannonball" Adderley once served as band director at Dillard High School in Fort Lauderdale. Julian moved to New York City in 1955 to pursue a master's degree, but soon began sitting in on alto saxophone with Oscar Pettiford's band at Café Bohemia. Julian drew inspiration from Charlie Parker and Benny Carter. He quickly attracted the attention of many great musicians, including Miles Davis in 1957. Julian played in the Miles Davis sextet for two years. Julian left the sextet to form other combos, including the Cannonball Adderley Sextet with his brother Nat on cornet. In the late sixties, this group achieved crossover success with pop audiences, notably without making artistic concessions. Cannonball died of a stroke in 1975 and is buried in Tallahassee.

- Singer/Songwriter Jimmy Buffett is a member of the Florida Artists Hall of Fame and lives in Key West.

Artists

- Florida is home to a number of famous collections of art including one owned by circus magnate John Ringling (Ringling Museum of Art).

- The Florida Artists Hall of Fame recognizes Florida natives and residents who made significant contributions to the arts in the state. Those who are inducted receive a bronze sculpture called *La Florida* by Enzo Torcolett, an artist in St. Augustine. These people include:

  - George Abbott – Director and Broadway legend – Lived in Miami Beach

Did You Know?

- St. Petersburg, Florida, is home to the largest collection of Salvador Dali art in the world.
- Art Deco is the primary architectural style found in South Miami Beach.
- The only museum in the U.S. dedicated to Latin American art and culture is the Florida Museum of Hispanic and Latin American Art in Coral Gables.

- Earl Cunningham – American Folk Artist – Self-taught painter who did a lot of landscapes and seascapes. At age thirteen he left his family and traveled up and down the coast before settling in St. Augustine.

- Doris Leeper – Sculptor and Painter – Founded the Atlantic Center for the Arts in New Smyrna Beach.

- Albin Polasek – Artist and Sculptor – Retired in Winter Park, Florida

- Jerry Uelsmann – Photographer – Retired in Gainesville

Did You Know?

Fernando Bujones, born in Miami, is regarded as one of the finest ballet dancers of the twentieth century and is hailed as the greatest American male dancer of his generation.

- The Orlando Museum of Art includes works by Georgia O'Keefe, Ansel Adams, John Singer Sargent, and John Chamberlain.

- The Appleton Museum of Art in Ocala was originally built to display the collection of Arthur I.

Floridians in Hollywood

Natives of Florida have made their mark on the big and small screen for many generations.

- Donald Trump owns Mar-A-Lago, an Italian-style mansion in Palm Beach. It used to be the acclaimed estate of Marjorie Merriweather Post, the heiress of the cereal company.

- Butterfly McQueen was born in Tampa in 1911. Butterfly (a stage name) was a dancer and actress. In 1939, she was cast as Prissy in *Gone with the Wind*. Her lines from that movie made sure that she would be remembered as a cultural icon. After

Did You Know?

Mickey Rourke used to box in Davie, Florida. As an actor, he played in <u>1941</u>, <u>The Outsiders</u>, and <u>Diner</u>.

all, few people can forget Prissy's declaration that she "don't know nothin' 'bout birthin' no babies!" Unfortunately, Butterfly grew frustrated with the limitations she faced in the film industry because of her race and retired from the movies in 1947. She took a few roles after that but nothing that would match her *Gone with the Wind* fame. Butterfly died in Georgia in 1995.

• Charles Joseph Scarborough of MSNBC's *Scarborough Country* went to Pensacola Catholic High School.

• Long before he made television history with *I Love Lucy*, and other sitcom creations, Desi Arnaz (1917-1986) was a resident of Florida. His family fled Cuba when Desi was just a teenager following the revolution that brought Fulgencio Batista to power. Desi worked as a musician and even brought the Conga Line to the U.S. before he met Lucille Ball and the two began work in television. Desi was always very grateful to America for providing him with so many opportunities. He even thanked the U.S. in his memoirs.

• *Good Times* actress Esther Rolle and pornographer Al Goldstein once lived in Pompano Beach.

Did You Know?

Desi Arnaz's best friend growing up was Al Capone Jr.

- In 1927, Sidney Poitier was born in Miami. His parents were from the Bahamas, and this heritage was very important to Sidney. He has had an extensive and remarkable acting career that includes such influential films as *Guess Who's Coming to Dinner*, about an interracial romance, *A Raisin in the Sun*, *In the Heat of the Night*, and the much loved *Sneakers*. In 1963, Sidney became the first African American to win an Academy Award when he took home the best actor prize for his role in *Lilies of the Field*. He was even knighted by the Queen of England in 2000 (which was also a nod to his Bahamian citizenship).

- Born in Bascom, Florida, Faye Dunaway is an alumna of the University of Florida. In 1967, Faye got her big break when she made the movie *Bonnie & Clyde* and also earned her first Oscar nomination. Although she didn't win that year, she would in 1977 for her role in *Network*. In 1981, she made the movie *Mommie Dearest* about former Hollywood star Joan Crawford. Faye is well remembered for that iconic role, but also blames the movie for the decline her career took afterwards. It was hard for audiences to see Faye as anyone other than Joan Crawford.

- Wrestler "Hulk" Hogan has a home in Clearwater.

- Harry Wayne Casey—of KC and the Sunshine Band—lives in Hialeah.

- Delta Burke was born in 1956 in Orlando. In 1974, she was crowned Miss Florida and went on to compete in the Miss America pageant. Delta is probably best remembered for her role on *Designing Women*. As Suzanne Sugarbaker, Delta made audiences laugh for years before leaving the show in 1991. She is also married to former *Major Dad* star Gerald McRaney. (The two met when McRaney guest starred as one of the fictious ex-husbands of Suzanne Sugarbaker.)

Did You Know?

Delta Burke claimed her mother got her name from a crazy household pet—the family cat!

- Even though he wasn't born in Florida, Burt Reynolds called Palm Beach home for many years. His father was the police chief there. Burt even maintains a home in Jupiter, Florida, today.

Did You Know?

Supposedly Burt's home in Jupiter was once a hideout for Al Capone.

- Catherine Keener is from Miami. You might have seen her in movies like *Being John Malkovich* or *The 40-Year-Old Virgin*.

- Plantation Hall in Plantation, Florida, was the backdrop for part of *There's Something About Mary*.

- Did you know that all of the following movies were filmed in or set in Florida? There was even a time when Florida was known as "Hollywood East."

Tarzan Finds a Son! (1938)

Lassie (1943)

Key Largo (1948)

Revenge of the Creature (1954)

Easy to Love (1954)

Flipper (1963 and 1996)

The Godfather: Part II (1974)

Scarface (1983)

Bad Boys (1995)

Any Given Sunday (1999)

Out of Time (2003)

2 Fast 2 Furious (2003)

Miami Vice (2006)

- Of course, Florida is also the setting for many well-known television shows. Let's not forget about:

Sea Hunt (1958-1961)

Flipper (1964-1968 and 1995-2000)

Miami Vice (1984-1989)

The Golden Girls (1985-1992)

I Dream of Jeannie (1965-1970)

The Written Word

Not only has Florida influenced visual art and music, but the state has left its mark on the world of literature as well.

- A very influential author of the Harlem Renaissance, Zora Neale Hurston was born in Eatonville in 1891. Zora eventually traveled north to study at Howard University in Washington, D.C., as well as pursue other interests like dance. In 1937, her novel *Their Eyes Were Watching God* was published. Unfortunately, Zora did not live to see the acclaim or respect her writing would evoke. Few people paid attention to the book at the time, and Zora died with no money to her name. In 1975, Alice Walker, another female writer and author of *The Color Purple*, revived interest in Zora's work and today *Their Eyes Were Watching God* is a standard in many literature classes.

- Florida's Poet Laureate is Dr. Edmund Skellings, appointed by Governor Bob Graham in 1980. The previous year, he was nominated for a Nobel Prize in Literature and for a Pulitzer Prize. Poet Laureates have no set term and are not compensated.

- Much of the James Bond novel *Live and Let Die* is set in St. Petersburg.

- Children's author Elaine Konigsburg has written eighteen books while living in Jacksonville. Today she lives in Ponte Vedra Beach. She was inducted into the Florida Artists Hall of Fame in 2000.

- Crime novelist John D. Macdonald has written many short stories, articles, and novels featuring Florida's culture and environment. He wrote a series of Travis McGee books, which were all set in Florida. *Condominium* is a novel set in the Florida Keys. It was written by MacDonald in 1977.

- Novelist Carl Hiassen was born in Plantation, Florida.

- Although the following writers weren't born in Florida, the state certainly influenced their writing:

  - Ernest Hemingway maintained a home in Key West.

Ernest Hemingway's house
Courtesy of VISIT FLORIDA

- Marjorie Kinnan Rawlings spent most of her life in rural Florida. The landscape there greatly influenced her Pulitzer prize winning novel *The Yearling*.

- Dave Barry was born in New York, but his writing got the country's attention during his time as a columnist with *The Miami Herald*.

- Playwright Tennessee Williams, who wrote *The Glass Menagerie*, moved to Key West in 1949 and lived there for more than thirty years. It was there that he wrote *Memoirs*. While in Florida, he received many honors including the Pulitzer Prize for *Cat on a Hot Tin Roof*.

- James Weldon Johnson was born in Jacksonville in 1871. After graduating from what is now Clark Atlanta University, he served as principal of Stanton, a school for African American students in Jacksonville. He moved to New York City in 1902 to work in musical theater. He later became a prominent figure in the Harlem Renaissance and one of the first African American professors at New York University. One of the works for which he is best known is *God's Trombones: Seven Negro Sermons in Verse*. Published in 1927, it celebrates the tradition of the folk preacher.

SPORTS AND RECREATION

Athletics in Florida

- Daytona Beach is home to popular motorcycle events Bike Week and Biketoberfest. Hundreds of thousands of bikers from all over the country travel to the city. Auto and motorcycle races were first held on the smooth beaches in 1902 and it was later nicknamed "The Birthplace of Speed."

- Bobby Bowden is one of the most well-known coaches in college football today. He has been the coach at Florida State University for thirty years. He has two national championships under his belt—one in 1993 and another in 1999.

- The Shuffleboard Hall of Fame is in St. Petersburg.

- Miami is the hometown of the Florida Marlins, Florida's professional baseball team.

- The Tampa Bay Lightning and Florida Panthers are Florida's professional hockey teams.

- When it comes to professional basketball, Florida has two teams—the Orlando Magic and the Miami Heat. Of course, these two cities have WNBA teams as well—the Orlando Miracle and Miami Sol.

- Florida has three NFL teams: the Jacksonville Jaguars, Tampa Bay Buccaneers, and Miami Dolphins.

- Two famous athletes are natives of Fort Walton Beach—Heisman Trophy Winner and quarterback Danny Wuerffel and National Football League kicker Jason Elam. Wuerffel won the Heisman Trophy in 1996 while playing for the University of Florida. Elam is best known for his fifty-one-yard field goal during Super Bowl XXXII, which was the second longest field goal ever kicked in a Super Bowl game. He currently is a place kicker for the Denver Broncos.

- Florida is home to fourteen professional soccer teams: Miami FC, Ajax Orlando Prospects, Bradenton Academics, Central Florida Craze,

Cocoa Expos, Palm Beach Pumas, Bradenton Athletics, Central Florida Crush, Central Florida Strikers, Miami Surf, Orlando Falcons, Palm Beach United, South Florida Breeze, and Tampa Bay United.

- Daytona is home to one of the largest NASCAR races in the country.

- Cuba first showed the game Jai Alai to Florida.

- Florida is the site of a number of Major League Baseball teams' spring training:

  - Atlanta Braves – Walt Disney World

  - Baltimore Orioles – Fort Lauderdale

  - Boston Red Sox – Fort Myers

  - Cincinnati Reds – Sarasota

  - Cleveland Indians – Winter Haven

  - Detroit Tigers – Lakeland

  - Florida Marlins – Jupiter

  - Houston Astros – Kissimmee

  - Kansas City Royals – Haines City

Did You Know?

Haines City is known as The Heart of Florida.

- LA Dodgers – Vero Beach

- Minnesota Twins – Fort Myers

- New York Mets – Port St. Lucie

- New York Yankees – Tampa

- Philadelphia Phillies – Clearwater

- Pittsburgh Pirates – Bradenton

- St. Louis Cardinals – Jupiter

- Tampa Bay Devil Rays – St. Petersburg

- Toronto Blue Jays – Dunedin

- Washington Nationals – Viera

Famous Florida Athletes

- Steve Spurrier was born in Miami in 1945. In high school, Steve played many sports, but by the time he went to college, he was focusing entirely on football. In 1966, Steve won the Heisman Trophy, the highest honor for any college football player.  After his own playing career ended, Steve went into coaching. He held many assistant and head coaching positions at schools like Duke University before making a name for himself as head coach at his former alma mater, the University of Florida. In 1996, Steve led the Gators to a national championship with a win over Florida State. In 2001, Steve surprised many Florida fans by accepting a coaching job with the Washington Redskins. At the time, the coaching contract he negotiated was the largest in NFL history. Unfortunately, Steve did not achieve as much success as a pro coach as he had during his days at Florida and eventually resigned. Today, Steve is the head coach at the University of South Carolina.

• Emmitt Smith went to Escambia High School in Pensacola, Florida.

• World record holder and sprinter Justin Gatlin attended Woodham High School in Pensacola.

• Steve Carlton was born in Miami in 1944. Steve had a twenty-three year career in baseball, most of which he spent with the Philadelphia Phillies. His nickname was "Lefty" because he was a left-handed pitcher. Steve won the Cy Young Award many times during his career, and for a while was locked in a battle with Nolan Ryan to see who would lead the league in strikeouts. In 1994, Steve was added to the Baseball Hall of Fame.

• Olympic Speedskaters Anthony Lobello and Jennifer Rodriguez are both Florida natives. Anthony is from Tallahassee and Jennifer is from Miami.

• Jerome McDougle of the Philadelphia Eagles once lived in Pompano Beach.

• Born in Key West in 1965, David Robinson went on to become one of the greatest basketball players the game has ever seen. His father was a military man, so David entered the Naval Academy after his high school graduation and first played basketball on the national stage as a member of Annapolis' college team. After graduation, a 7'1" David was signed to the San Antonio Spurs but had to fulfill two years of military service before joining the team. In his first year in the NBA, David was named Rookie of the Year. David was on the 1992 U.S. Olympic team that won a gold medal, and he finally realized his dream of an NBA championship during his last year with the Spurs in 2003. Today, David focuses on church and community in his efforts to help those around him.

Did You Know?

David Robinson's nickname is "The Admiral." The name refers to his time in the U.S. Navy, but his actual rank was far below that of admiral. He retired as a lieutenant junior grade.

- Born in Tampa in 1964, Dwight Gooden went on to become one of the most feared pitchers in the National League in the eighties. Throughout his short career, Dwight played for the Mets, Yankees, Indians, Astros, and Devil Rays. He was Rookie of the Year in 1984, and received the Cy Young Award in 1985. Dwight tested positive for cocaine during spring training in 1987, and again in 1994 and 1995. It was this drug abuse that lead to his premature demise. He retired in 2001 after he was cut from the Yankees during spring training.

Florida Recreation

- More tourists flock to Orlando for roller coasters and other amusement park attractions than any other city in the country.

- In 1971, Walt Disney World opened. Its first year, only ten thousand people visited the amusement park. Now, more than ten thousand people visit Walt Disney World every hour.

- It cost $400,000,000 to open Disney World.

- Disney World is double the size of Manhattan!

- Weeki Wachee gives underwater shows of *The Little Mermaid* by Hans Christian Anderson. They have since 1947.

- Gatorland is home to the most alligators in the world.

- Epcot is often called the "thinking man's theme park."

Did You Know?

- Florida athletics is a $16 billion industry.

- Florida has more than 1,200 golf courses.

- Florida has nearly 3.5 million registered fishermen.

- Florida has an adult flag football program.

- Parrot Jungle in Miami is an excellent place to see some of Florida's wildlife.

- Lion Country Safari lets you experience all of the wildlife of the African landscape from the safety of your car.

- But, if you want to narrow down that wildlife, Monkey Jungle might be right for you.

- Where do you find orcas in Florida? Sea World Orlando of course.

- If you want to experience the wonders of space from this planet, visit the Kennedy Space Center.

Kennedy Space Center
Courtesy of VISIT FLORIDA

- Busch Gardens is a wonderful place to visit in Florida. You might know it better by its nickname, "The Dark Continent."

- Ripley's Believe it or Not Museum can be found in St. Augustine.

- Where in Florida can you experience flight firsthand with hot air balloon rides or flight lessons? Fantasy of Flight in central Florida.

- Where can you stay in an underwater hotel? At Jules' Underwater Sea Lodge in Key Largo.

- Metrozoo opened in 1981.

- If you love the Big Top, don't miss Ringling's Circus Museum.

- Universal Studio's Islands of Adventure lets visitors "live the adventure."

- The Boggy Bayou Mullet Festival is held annually in Niceville.

- Florida is home to a handful of historic homes available for touring. They include:

  - Majorie Kinnan Rawlings State Historic Site – Hawthrone – Home of the Pulitzer Prize winning author who wrote *The Yearling*. Her old typewriter is still on the table by the porch.

- Mary McLeod Bethune Cottage – Daytona Beach – Simple home of the educator and advisor to Franklin D. Roosevelt.

- Whitehall – Palm Beach – 1902 mansion of railroad tycoon Henry Flagler showcasing a railroad car on the property.

Whitehall
Courtesy of VISIT FLORIDA

- The Edison Home Museum in Fort Myers houses many of Thomas Edison's first inventions. The building was once his winter home.

Thomas Edison's Home

- Islamorada is billed as the sports fishing capital of the world.

- Key Largo is the dive capital of the world.

- The Pinellas Trail, a 47-mile hiking/biking trail, connects St. Petersburg with north Pinellas County, and is the longest urban linear trail in the eastern U.S.

STATE
POLITICS

A Glimpse at Government

- The government of Florida is broken up into three branches—legislative, judicial, and executive.

- Florida's legislature has a Senate with 40 members and a House of Representatives with 120 members.

- Florida has twenty-seven electoral college votes, two Senators, and twenty-five elected officials in the House of Representatives.

- Florida was once 68.5 percent Democrat, but more conservative voters have recently moved into the state.

- Florida is always considered to be a key swing state in presidential elections.

Did You Know?

Janet Reno, the first woman Attorney General of the United States, was born in Miami. She was a debating champion and valedictorian of Coral Gables High School.

- Florida's legislature is part-time, and meets only sixty regular day sessions per year. When special sessions are needed, they are called by the governor.

- House of Representative members serve two-year terms. Senators from the state serve four-year terms. Members of both houses are limited to a maximum of eight years of service.

Influential Political Figures

- The first man in charge of Florida was governor before the territory was even officially made a state! You might recognize his name, too—Andrew Jackson. Eventually he became U.S. president, and he was a widely recognized military hero in his day. Jackson was named as the first governor of Florida in 1821. He distinguished himself during many battles over the American frontier and was especially known for leading the Battle of New Orleans during the War of 1812.

- Sidney Johnston Catts won the governorship of Florida in 1917. What's interesting about Sidney is that he was a member of the short-lived Prohibition political party. (Prohibitionists wanted to do away with alcohol, and briefly succeeded in that goal when a Constitutional amendment was passed to that affect in 1919. It was repealed in

1933.) Only two members of the Prohibition party were ever elected to political seats, and Sidney was one of them.

• John Ellis "Jeb" Bush was born in Texas in 1953. He was the 43rd governor of Florida. His father was U.S. president from 1988 to 1992, and his brother is currently serving his second term in the White House. Of course, you might have seen Jeb on the news during the presidential election of 1999. During that year, as Al Gore and George W. Bush were battling over the presidency, the votes in Florida became crucial to deciding the outcome of the election. There is speculation as to whether or not Jeb will run for president someday, too.

A Timeline of Governors

The following is a list of Florida's governors before and since it became a state. How many of the names do you recognize?

Military Governors

Andrew Jackson (1821)

Territory Governors

William P. Duval (1822-1834)

John Eaton (1834-1836)

Richard K. Call (1836-1839)

Robert R. Reid (1839-1841)

Richard K. Call (1841-1844)

John Branch (1844-1845)

State Governors

William D. Moseley (1845-1849)

Thomas Brown (1849-1853)

James E. Broome (1853-1857)

Madison S. Perry (1857-1861)

John Milton (1861-1865)

Abraham K. Allison (1865)

William Marvin (1865)

David S. Walker (1865-1868)

Harrison Reed (1868-1873)

Ossian B. Hart (1873-1874)

Marcellus L. Sterns (1874-1877)

George F. Drew (1877-1881)

Did You Know?

- Only four governors on this list have served two full terms in office: Reubin O'D. Askew, D. Robert Graham, Lawton M. Chiles Jr., and Jeb Bush.

- J. Wayne Mixson was governor for the shortest period of time. He served only three days in office!

William D. Bloxham (1881-1885)

Edward A. Perry (1885-1889)

Francis P. Fleming (1889-1893)

Henry L. Mitchell (1893-1897)

William D. Bloxham (1897-1901)

William S. Jennings (1901-1905)

Napolean B. Broward (1905-1909)

Albert W. Gilchrist (1909-1913)

Park Trammell (1913-1917)

Sidney J. Catts (1917-1921)

Cary A. Hardee (1921-1925)

John W. Martin (1925-1929)

Doyle E. Carlton (1929-1933)

David Sholtz (1933-1937)

Fred P. Cone (1937-1941)

Spessard Holland (1941-1945)

Millard F. Caldwell (1945-1949)

Fuller Warren (1949-1953)

Daniel T. McCarty (1953)

Charley E. Johns (1953-1955)

T. LeRoy Collins (1955-1961)

C. Farris Bryant (1961-1965)

W. Haydon Burns (1965-1967)

Claude R. Kirk Jr. (1967-1971)

Reubin O'D. Askew (1971-1979)

D. Robert Graham (1979-1987)

J. Wayne Mixson (1987)

Robert Martinez (1987-1991)

Lawton M. Chiles Jr. (1991-1998)

Kenneth H. MacKay Jr. (1998-1999)

John E. Bush (1999-2007)

Charles J. Crist Jr. (2007-)

COLLEGES AND UNIVERSITIES

Florida's Universities

There are plenty of schools and universities throughout Florida. You might recognize some of Florida's graduates listed below with their schools.

- The University of Florida was founded in Gainesville in 1905. It is the largest university in the state of Florida and the fourth largest university in the whole United States. Today, it has just under fifty thousand students!

- Bob Vila, Jesse Palmer, Darrell Hammond, Forrest Sawyer, Mel Tillis, Josh Fogg, Jason Williams, Emmitt Smith, Steve Spurrier, and Melinda Lou "Wendy" Thomas all graduated from the University of Florida. (Wendy Thomas is Dave Thomas' daughter. He named the Wendy's fast food chain after her.)

- Although the University of Florida might be the biggest college in the state, Florida State University (FSU) is older. Thomas Jefferson's grandson,

Mayor Francis W. Eppes, helped get the school going in 1857.

- FSU has seventeen colleges and campuses in Panama City and Sarasota in addition to the main campus in Tallahassee.

- Burt Reynolds, Christine Lahti, Terry Bowden, Richard Simmons, Jim Morrison, and Deion Sanders all went to FSU.

- The University of Miami is located in Coral Gable and was founded in 1925. The school's official colors are taken from the orange tree—they are green, orange, and white. With just over fifteen thousand students today, the University of Miami is a well-ranked private university known for its athletics program (the Hurricanes) as well as having graduate programs in law and medicine.

- Famous alumni from the University of Miami include Sylvester Stallone, Ray Liotta, Gloria Estefan, Enrique Iglesias, Ken Dorsey, Warren Sapp, and Jill Arrington.

- Rollins College is the oldest recognized college in Florida. It was founded in 1885, when New England Congregationalists wanted to bring their style of education down South. You might have heard of the type of education they wanted to spread—it was the liberal arts. The school's motto reflects its religious roots. It's "Fiat Lux" or "Let There be Light" from Genesis.

- Rollins graduates include Anthony Perkins (from the original *Psycho* film) and the PBS children's programming staple and host of *Mr. Rogers' Neighborhood*, Fred Rogers.

- Of course Gatorade originally comes from Florida. It was named for the school mascot where it was invented—the University of Florida's Gators.

- Florida's first private university was Stetson University, founded by Henry A. Deland and originally called Deland University. Later, the name was changed to honor John B. Stetson, a famous hat manufacturer and supporter of the school. Stetson is located between Daytona Beach and Orlando.

- In 1900, Stetson became home to the first law school in the state of Florida.

- Stetson was also the first white university in Florida to be integrated.

- Business mogul Charles E. Merrill graduated from Stetson. He helped found the Merrill Lynch financial corporation.

- Here are just a few of the other schools located in Florida:
  - Barry University
  - Eckerd College
  - Edison College
  - Florida A & M University
  - Florida Atlantic University
  - Florida Southern College
  - Jacksonville University
  - Miami Dade College
  - St. Thomas University
  - Trinity College of Florida
  - Webber College

GRAB BAG

What's in a Name?

The names of many cities in Florida have interesting origins.

- Fernandina Beach in Nassau County is named after Cuba, which was originally named Fernandina.

- The city of Boca Raton is from the Spanish phrase "Boca de Ratones," meaning "rat's mouth." This was a term used by sailors describing hidden rocks in the ocean that their ship's cable could accidentally bump against.

- Orlando is the largest inland city in Florida. The city's nickname is The City Beautiful, but a contest may soon change that.

- Translated from the Seminole, Hypoluxo's (the city's) name means "water all round—no get out."

- Florida has a city named after a major holiday. It's Christmas, Florida.

- Naples, Florida, is named after Naples, Italy.

Miami skyline
Courtesy of VISIT FLORIDA

- Ironically sunny, St. Petersburg is named after a city of the same name in Russia— which is one of the coldest places in the world.

- "Miami" comes from the name "Mayaimi," which means "very large."

- Clearwater, Florida, was likely named after a fresh water spring that used to flow where City Hall now stands.

- Some historians believe that the city of Orlando is named after a soldier who died during a battle against a Seminole Indian Tribe. However, Orlando Reeves was simply a sugar mill operator. When settlers found his name carved in a tree, they just assumed it was his grave. They began calling the area "Orlando's grave" and later "Orlando."

Did You Know?

Charlotte Harbor is the point where the Peace River meets the ocean.

- Jacksonville is the most populated city in the state and the thirteenth most populated city in the U.S. It was originally named Cowford after the narrow part of the St. Johns River where cattle would cross. It was renamed in 1822 for Andrew Jackson, who was the first military governor of the Florida Territory and later the seventh President of the United States.

- Punta Gorda gets its name from its size and location. The city's name translates to "Fat Point" from Spanish because a broad part of the land juts into Charlotte Harbor.

State Trivia

Here's some more information about Florida we'll bet you didn't know!

- *The National Enquirer* is based out of Lantana, Florida.

- Ransom E. Olds, the man responsible for the Oldsmobile, also founded a city. It's Oldsmar, Florida.

- Hialeah, Florida, is the number one city in the U.S. where Spanish is spoken. More than 90 percent of the population primarily speaks Spanish.

- The biggest strawberry shortcake was baked in Plant City, the Winter Strawberry Capital of the World. It even made the *Guinness Book of World Records*!

- The Annual Mug Race is the longest sailboat race that takes place on a river. It is a forty-two-mile event from Palatka to Jacksonville on the St. Johns River.

- The Orlando International Airport was built partially out of the McCoy Air Force Base, which closed in 1974.

- The supposed Shark Tooth Capital of the World is Venice, Florida.

- In 1926, Pan Am Airlines was started in Key West.

- Amelia Island, in the northeast corner of Florida, was once claimed by eight different countries at once. It is the only U.S. territory to have ever served under eight flags.

- There is a rather famous gravestone in Key West, Florida. It reads, "I told you I was sick."

- While the most common language spoken at home is English, in 2000, 16.5 percent of Florida residents spoke Spanish and 2.2 percent of Florida residents spoke French.

- After it was finished in 1989, the Dame Point Bridge was the longest cable-stayed bridge in the U.S., the longest concrete span in the Western Hemisphere, and the third longest cable-stayed bridge in the world.

- The "headquarters" for the church of Scientology is located in Clearwater. It was founded in the

1970s when a group bought the Fort Harrison Hotel for $3 million.

- Clearwater Beach was once home to a giant hoax about a Bigfoot. Students from Clearwater High School decided to form some fake footprints in the sand, and not long after they were discovered, news of the unique prints were reported in several local newspapers. The students kept quiet, and it wasn't until twenty years later that one of them came forward and admitted the hoax.

- In 1996, a religious group put a large image of the Virgin Mary on the side of an office building that used to be a bank. When eighteen-year-old Kyle Maskell decided to play a joke on the group by breaking three of the windows, his guilt got the best of him and he confessed. He paid the ministry $1,200 for repairs and spent ten days in jail.

- There are 1,473 miles of interstate highway in Florida.

- The only time Miami Beach has ever seen snow was in February 1978.

- Ron Jon Surf Shop in Cocoa Beach is the largest surf shop in the world.

- In 1927, Daytona Beach was dubbed the World's Most Famous Beach.

- Ponce de Leon Inlet Light Station is one of the best preserved lighthouses in the nation. It was originally completed in 1887 and is visited by 100,000 tourists a year.

Ponce de Leon Inlet Light Station
Courtesy of VISIT FLORIDA

- South Beach, Miami, is often referred to as SoBe.

- South Beach was originally a coconut farm, but the first house was built on the beach in 1886. It wasn't until 1920 that the city started booming when moguls like J.C. Penney and Harvey Firestone moved in.

- In 1838, the Amelia Lighthouse was transported brick by brick from Cumberland Island. It is located farther inland than any other lighthouse in Florida.

- Prime fashion photography season in South Beach is from October through March.

- Florida was once the top filmmaking state in the U.S.

- *The New York Times* once reported that Fort Lauderdale first became a Spring Break hotspot when the men's swimming team from Colgate University traveled there to practice in 1935. In 1981, twenty thousand students vacationed there for Spring Break.

- Watch out when you're in Clearwater, Florida. More people are struck by lightning there than anywhere else in the United States.

- The Sunshine Skyway Bridge gives drivers unobstructed views of Tampa Bay.

- Florida has the highest average precipitation of any state.

- The highest point of peninsular Florida is Sugarloaf Mountain in Lake County.

- Florida is the fifth largest producer of greenhouse gases.

- Oklahoma City bomber Timothy McVeigh once lived in Plantation, Florida.

- At the National Museum of Naval Aviation, one of the largest air and space museums in the world, you can fly a Desert Storm mission in a flight simulator. The museum also features four Blue Angel A-4 Skyhawks in a diving diamond formation in a seven-story glass atrium.

National Museum of Naval Aviation
Courtesy of VISIT FLORIDA

- The Blue Angels are stationed at Naval Air Station Pensacola during show season.